Retur

Plea

may

rec

SURVIVING
IN A WORLD
WITHOUT
WATER

MADELINE TYLER

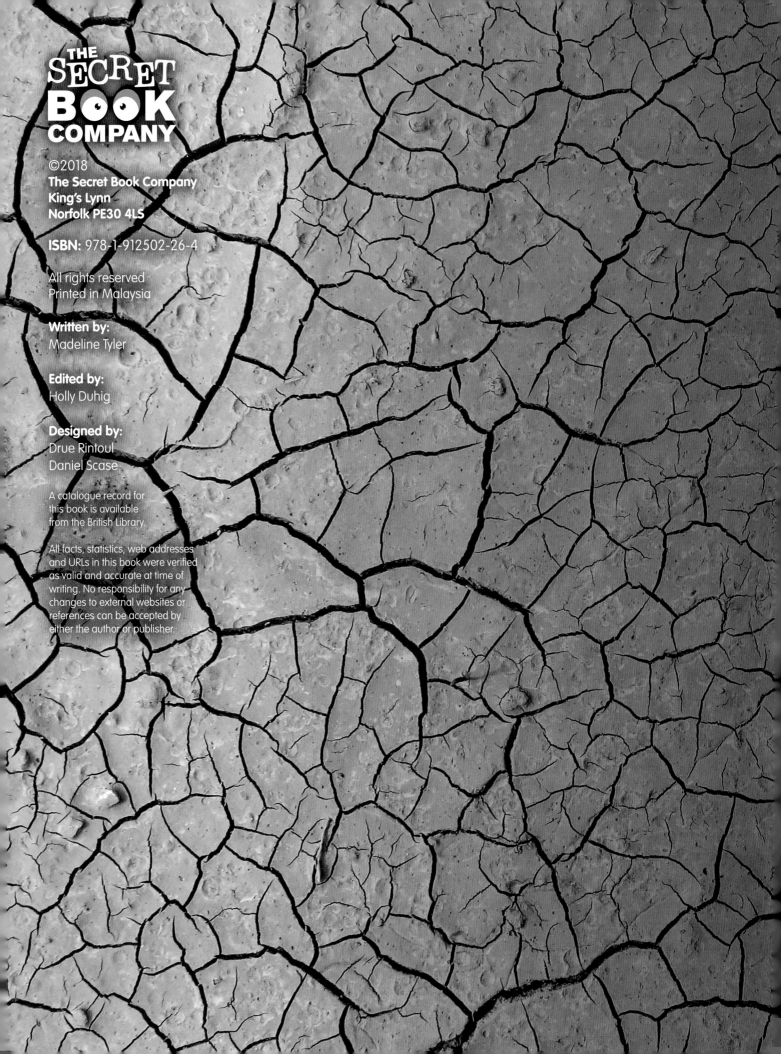

THE SECRET BOOK COMPANY

©2018
The Secret Book Company
King's Lynn
Norfolk PE30 4LS

ISBN: 978-1-912502-26-4

Written by:
Madeline Tyler

Edited by:
Holly Duhig

Designed by:
Drue Rintoul
Daniel Scase

CONTENTS

Words that look like THIS can be found in the glossary on page 31.

WHERE'S ALL THE WATER?

We use water every day in all parts of our lives. We drink it, wash with it, and even use it to flush the toilet. Can you imagine a world without water? What would you drink? How would you wash? Most importantly, how would you flush the toilet? This nightmare could soon become a reality for cities all around the world as the rain stops falling and the **RESERVOIRS** dry up. There'll be no more water fights or trips to the swimming pool, no hot (or cold!) baths, and you may have to get used to having dirty clothes too. Living without water will affect everything we do, and it definitely won't be easy. You'll have to learn to become creative and **RESOURCEFUL** and discover how to find water in some very unexpected places.

When the world runs out of water, there'll be lots of panic and it might not be very clear how or why it's happened. Everyone will be rushing to get their hands on the last few bottles of water left in the supermarket. Fights might break out and wars may even be started over who gets the last bottle on the shelf. Remember, there's strength in numbers, so stick with your friends and family and you'll stand a better chance of surviving. If you all work together and share your **RESOURCES**, it might not be so bad.

DROUGHTS

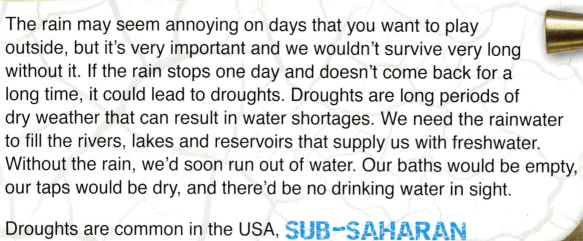

The rain may seem annoying on days that you want to play outside, but it's very important and we wouldn't survive very long without it. If the rain stops one day and doesn't come back for a long time, it could lead to droughts. Droughts are long periods of dry weather that can result in water shortages. We need the rainwater to fill the rivers, lakes and reservoirs that supply us with freshwater. Without the rain, we'd soon run out of water. Our baths would be empty, our taps would be dry, and there'd be no drinking water in sight.

Droughts are common in the USA, **SUB-SAHARAN** Africa, and Australia, but can occur at any time and anywhere in the world. We rely on the rain to water the earth, so many crops fail and many people go hungry during a drought. With no food and no water, survival in a drought is difficult.

EARTHQUAKES

Even if you get lots of rain, it doesn't mean that it will make its way to the plumbing in your house. Droughts can leave you with no water, but so can natural disasters like earthquakes. After a powerful earthquake, pipes and waterways can end up damaged from the shaking earth. Water supplies may be shut off to prevent any flooding from burst or damaged pipes. This could leave your city without water for weeks or even months. Most people can't last any longer than a week without water so, whether it's a drought, an earthquake, or something else, read this guide carefully. It'll teach you everything there is to know about surviving in a world without water.

This guide contains lots of useful skills and advice, so keep it near and don't lose it — who knows when it could save your life!

DON'T SWEAT IT

When you first hear the announcement that the world is running out of water, you will probably panic. The news will be scary and confusing, and you may not know what to do. Questions might run through your head, making you worry even more: where has the water gone? When will it come back? How will you survive?

You and your family might start screaming, crying or running up and down the city looking for water before it all disappears. However, this is the worst thing you can do. Crying and shouting will make your body lose water which could quickly make you **DEHYDRATED**. Try to control your breathing and keep your mouth shut. This might be hard if you're a chatterbox, but it could help you stay alive for a bit longer until you find something to drink.

See page 28 for more information about dehydration.

Walking, running and exercising all use energy and can make you very sweaty. Normally, this is OK because you can drink lots of water to replace the water you lose from your sweat. However, in a world without water, this is more difficult. You'll sweat and sweat and sweat until there's no water left in your body. Eventually you'll become really thirsty but there'll be nothing for you to drink. Stay as still as you can to reduce the sweating and hopefully you won't be so thirsty.

Meditation and yoga are great ways to stay calm. It'll help you to take slow, deep breaths and stay very still and very silent. See how long you can stay in the 'easy pose' for – time might even pass faster than you expect!

Easy Pose

WATER RATIONS

Before the water runs out completely, **GOVERNMENTS** might announce day zero, which is when everyone's water supplies are turned off to save whatever water is left. Water rations might be introduced to control how much water everyone uses. Rationing is when something, like water, is shared equally amongst lots of people. This makes sure that everyone has a little bit every day and that the **RESERVES** don't run dry.

MINISTRY **MF** OF FOOD

RATION BOOK

Surname..............................

Other Names..........................

Address..............................
(as on Identity Card)

Date of birth (Day).......... (Month).......... (Year)..........

R.B.4 — 7   JUNIOR

NATIONAL REGISTRATION NUMBER

FOOD OFFICE CODE No.

J

N.   D
M.F.

~ 8.17

Serial No. of Ration Book

EJ 115019

IF FOUND RETURN TO ANY FOOD OFFICE

You might be given a ration book or ration card that tells you how much water you'll be given each time. You can take these to the water stations and exchange them for a little bit of water every day. Remember to always bring your ration book or ration cards when you visit the water station, and never use someone else's. This could get you in a lot of trouble.

If you're lucky, you should be able to collect 50 litres of water a day. You'll have to use this water for drinking, washing, cooking, and for anything else that you normally use water for. 50 litres might sound like a lot, but most people use over 150 litres every single day! After you've bathed, flushed the toilet, and cleaned all your clothes, you might be surprised at how quickly your ration disappears.

Some people, like your smelly older brother, will need more than 50 litres a day, and other people will need a lot less. It might be a good idea for you and your family to share your rations with each other. This way, if you have plenty of water, you can help someone else out.

To survive on your new water ration, you will have to change the way you live. Keep reading this guide to find out how.

TURN OFF THE TAP

GETTING STINKY

Living on rations and only being able to use 50 litres of water a day can be really difficult. You'll have to keep track of all your ration cards and remember to collect the right ration every day. This is a lot to take in, but luckily there are a few things you can do to save some water around your house and make this new life a bit easier.

The first thing you can do is stop washing. Yes, that's right; no more showers, no more baths, and no more washing your clothes either. All of these use up far too much water so you'd better get used to being a bit smellier than usual. If your clothes get really stinky, try hanging them outside in the fresh air. They won't be clean, but hopefully they'll smell a bit better.

SHORT SHOWERS

If your family get so smelly that you need to wear a **GAS MASK** just to walk around the house, you may have to let them have a quick wash. When they're in the shower, they might get carried away and forget all about the rations, so stand guard outside the door with a timer. Set the timer for five minutes and make sure the taps are turned off as soon as the time is up. You don't want all of your drinking water to end up down the drain, so shout your countdown through the door to make sure they don't forget. If this doesn't work, you could try turning it into a competition to see who can have the shortest shower. Whoever wins could get a large glass of rationed water as the prize.

Always shower over a bucket to collect the **GREY WATER**. You can then reuse this water to wash your clothes.

13

PULL THE PLUG

Some of your family might say that they need a bath and not a shower, but whatever you do, don't listen to them. You'd need 80 litres just to fill up one bath – that's more than a whole day's ration! To stop your family from having sneaky baths while you're not there, collect up all of the bath plugs around your house and either hide them somewhere safe or throw them away. There are far more important things that you'll need your water rations for so, instead of wasting them on getting clean, try **STOCKPILING** as much as you can. No one knows when the water will be back so it's always best to prepare for the worst.

FLASH FLUSH

Believe it or not, flushing the toilet just once can use up to 13 litres of water. This is a lot of water to go to waste, so try to keep flushing to a minimum. While you're living on rations, you should only flush the toilet once a day, but if you need to flush it more often, use the grey water you saved from your shower. If you don't have any grey water nearby, you could put a brick in the tank of your toilet. This will help you to use less water every time you flush. This can be quite tricky, so always make sure you ask an adult to help you.

Remember: 'if it's yellow, let it mellow. If it's brown, flush it down!'

RAINWATER

Rations can only last for so long, and eventually all of the city's water reserves will be used up. When this happens, it doesn't mean that your chances of survival are over. As long as there's still rain falling, you'll still have access to plenty of water. Set up a rainwater tank next to your house and connect it to your **GUTTERING**. This will collect any rainwater that runs off your roof. You can use almost anything as your rainwater tank, but just make sure that it's big enough so that the water won't overflow and spill over the sides. You should also add a cover on top of your tank to stop any nasty bits from being blown into your clean, fresh water.

If you're living through a drought and rainfall is very rare, you'll need to collect as much water as you can to last you until it rains again. Empty your rainwater tank regularly and store the water in large bottles or containers that you can keep in your house. You and your family will have to be careful to make sure that you don't run out of water. If you're struggling, you could make a chart that shows exactly how much water everyone is allowed to use each day. This will help everyone to keep track of how much water they're using and how much is left.

HEAD DOWNHILL

When the rain does stop for good, survival will become even more difficult. The water you've saved up should keep you going for a little longer, but when this runs out you'll have to go out in search of some more. Water always flows downwards because of **GRAVITY**, so the best place to start is anywhere that's downhill. Try heading for **VALLEYS** or any low-lying areas like the bottom of a mountain, and any water left on Earth will trickle down to where you're waiting.

Before you head out into the wilderness, pack a bag with some handy supplies. Some binoculars, an emergency whistle, warm clothes and a torch could all be very useful. Don't forget some empty bottles and containers to collect your water in, too!

In a world that's running out of water, it might not be as easy as waiting for the water to come to you. If you've had no luck so far, search the area for any signs of water. Listen out for flowing rivers and streams but don't worry if you can't hear any. Keep an eye out for any dried **RIVERBEDS** too as these might actually be an unexpected source of water. Concentrate on bends in the river and look out for any dirt that looks darker than the rest. If you dig down into the ground, you should find some mud and wet earth. Keep digging and you'll reach water! Use a small container to collect as much water as you can before moving on to another spot.

19

FOLLOW THE ANIMALS

What about if there are no rivers or streams nearby? Or maybe there are but you just can't find them? If only there was someone or something that could show you the way and take you straight to the water source. Well, there is!

LOOK DOWN

Looking out for animals and their **TRACKS** is a quick and easy way to find water. Just like us, nearly all animals need a non-stop supply of water to stay alive. Animals are much better at surviving in the wild than humans are, and they're often a lot better at finding water, too. Many of them don't travel far and prefer to stay near to a place where they can get to water quickly. They'll often follow the same path to and from the river or lake that they drink from, so look out for a long trail made up of lots of tracks.

Wild boar can always be found very close to water, so if you see a wild boar track like this one, don't take another step! Have a look around you – the water is probably only a few metres away.

LOOK UP

While you're busy looking down at the ground, don't forget to keep one eye on what's going on in the sky. Look out for any birds flying overhead, especially pigeons. Pigeons fly towards a **WATERHOLE** in the evening, just before sunset, and fly back to their nests after they've had enough to drink. Look out for how the pigeons are flying and this will tell you whether they're on their way to the waterhole, or if they're heading back to their nests. If they are flying low and fast, they're heading for water, but if they're quite slow and stopping for a rest on the tops of trees, they're flying towards their nests. Only follow a fast-flying pigeon or you could end up heading in the wrong direction!

Swarms of insects, like mosquitoes, can also be a sign that there's water nearby.

TAP THE TREES

Although animals are very clever, they'll soon run out of water too. Eventually the waterholes will dry up, and there'll be no rivers or lakes in sight. Larger animals like wild boars and pigeons will die and you'll have to rely on much smaller creatures, like ants, to show you where you can find something to drink.

Lots of insects use the water that's hidden inside trees to stay alive. You won't be able to see this water, so you'll need to know what to look out for to find it. If you see a long line of insects heading in the same direction up a tree, then they're probably looking for water. Ants climb trees in a line, one after the other, and disappear into a hole. This shows you where to start looking for the water!

Once you've found a tree that definitely has some water inside, you'll need to know how to get it out. Whatever you do, don't chop any trees down. Instead, make a mop by tying a piece of cloth to the end of a stick. Dip the mop into the hole that the insects are climbing into and soak up all the water. Next, squeeze the cloth over one of your containers and voilà – you now have water!

Baobab Tree

Look out for baobab, wattle and she-oak trees as these have large pools of water inside their trunks. Baobab trees are the best, and some can even hold up to 120,000 litres inside their trunks! That's enough water to keep you going for months, so there's no chance of you getting thirsty.

WATER DOWSING

If there aren't any trees nearby, or none of them have enough water inside, then you may need to try a different method. Dowsing is a great way of finding water sources that are hidden deep under the ground. A 'Y' shaped stick is the best tool for water dowsing, but many people use keys or wire coat hangers, so just try to make the most of whatever you can get your hands on. Have a look around your house and garden and see if there's anything that would make a good dowsing tool. The best ones have a part that you can hold onto, like handles, and a long part that sticks out in front of you.

As you're getting the hang of dowsing, try practising in your garden. When you feel a bit more confident, explore a bit farther away. Hold your tool in two hands and point it slightly upwards. As you walk around an area, keep an eye on your tool: is it wobbling or moving up or down? You'll know when you're standing above a water source because the end of your tool will move from pointing upwards to pointing down towards the ground. When this happens, grab a shovel and start digging. If you're lucky, you'll find lots and lots of water, which will mean you can fill up a few bottles to store in your house. You can sell any spare bottles to your neighbours and earn a bit of money.

PURIFICATION

This guide has hopefully taught you lots of different ways that you can find water during a **SHORTAGE**. However, even if you are successful and you do find some, your problems aren't over. How can you make sure that the water you find out in the wilderness is clean and ready to drink? What if it's not safe? If you're not careful, dirty water can make you really, really ill. If you're collecting water from streams, trees, or dirty, muddy pits, you'll need to **PURIFY** it to remove anything that can cause disease, like **PARASITES** and **BACTERIA**. There are a few different ways you can do this, so grab a saucepan, a strainer and some branches from a pine tree – it's time to get to work!

FILTERING

The first thing you'll need to do is **FILTER** out any big bits that you can see in your water. Can you think of anything worse than taking a nice, big gulp to find that there's a spider swimming around in your mouth? Use a dish cloth or an old shirt as your strainer and pour the water through it into a container. Your water will look a bit cleaner now, but there's still some things in there that you can't see.

BOILING

To completely purify the water and remove any germs, you'll need to boil it. Heat it over a stove or a fire until you can see plenty of bubbles, then take it off the heat and wait for it to cool down again before drinking it.

If you're still not sure whether your water is safe to drink or not, you can use a pine branch to remove any leftover **PATHOGENS**. Take a branch from a pine tree and remove all of the bark. Pour the water slowly over the branch and you'll have clean water!

OPERATION REHYDRATION

Humans can't survive very long without water, and if you go any longer than three days without a drink, you could become dehydrated. Dehydration is when your body loses more liquids than it takes in. If you're dehydrated, it's important that you get a drink and **REHYDRATE** as quickly as you can. Look out for some common **SYMPTOMS** of dehydration so you can make sure that you save yourself before it's too late…

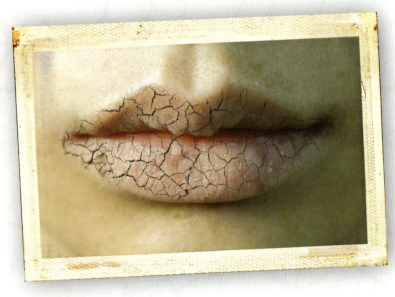

DRY YOUR EYES

Have you been feeling thirstier than usual? Or have you noticed that your mouth, lips and eyes are really, really dry and itchy? These are all early signs of dehydration so quickly try to find some water before it all disappears. It's important to keep your stores of water well-stocked so that, hopefully, you'll never get to this point.

NEED A NAP?

If you're feeling a bit tired and weak, it's not because you need an early night. Dehydration can make you feel sleepy but, whatever you do, don't take a nap. If you fall asleep with severe dehydration, you might not wake up again! Instead, sit down somewhere and take a few little sips of water until you feel a little bit better.

ACHES AND PAINS

As well as feeling LETHARGIC, you may notice some aches and pains all around your body. If your lower back hurts, or if you have pain in the JOINTS of your arms, legs, fingers and toes, this is a sure sign that you're dehydrated. Your muscles may also begin to cramp. You'll know if you have cramp because you'll feel a sharp pain in your muscle before it suddenly becomes very tight. Although these symptoms on their own aren't dangerous, dehydration can be.

29

SURVIVING IN A WORLD WITHOUT WATER

Congratulations – you've managed to survive in a world without water! It hasn't been easy, but you've learnt to become resourceful and find water in some unexpected places. The next few months will be difficult, but if you follow this guide then you should be okay. Store up all your rations and use them only when you really, really need to. If you do run out of water, then at least you'll know where and how to find some more. If you're smart, you and your family should have enough water to keep you going until the water comes back – if it ever does! By now, you must be an expert on living in a world with no water, so share your new knowledge and skills with your friends, family and neighbours. If everyone works together, then maybe it won't be so bad.

Remember to look out for the symptoms of dehydration and help anyone who's not looking so good.

GLOSSARY

BACTERIA	microscopic living things that can cause diseases
DEHYDRATED	when someone has lost a lot of water from their body
FILTER	remove or separate solids from liquids
GAS MASK	a mask worn on a person's face to protect from gases
GOVERNMENTS	the group of people with the authority to run a country and decide its laws
GRAVITY	the force that pulls everything downwards towards the centre of the Earth
GREY WATER	waste water from a home
GUTTERING	open pipes along the edge of a roof used to collect and carry rainwater
JOINTS	structures in the human body where two bones join together
LETHARGIC	to feel tired and without any energy
PARASITES	living things that live on or in another living thing. Parasites can sometimes cause disease
PATHOGENS	organisms that can cause disease in living things
PURIFY	to make clean, and free from anything bad
REHYDRATE	to stop something or someone from being dehydrated by giving them water
RESERVES	things, such as materials, saved for a particular purpose
RESERVOIRS	natural chambers that hold liquid, such as water
RESOURCEFUL	to deal with difficult situations quickly and creatively
RESOURCES	supplies of things like money, materials or water
RIVERBEDS	the bottoms of rivers where water flows through
SHORTAGE	not enough of something
STOCKPILING	the act of saving a supply of materials
SUB-SAHARAN	in Africa, south of the Sahara
SYMPTOMS	things that happen in the body suggesting that there is a disease or disorder
TRACKS	the marks left on the ground by the feet of animals
VALLEYS	long, narrow and deep grooves in the land, usually between hills or mountains
WATERHOLE	a low part in the ground where water collects

INDEX

Photo Credits: Images are courtesy of Shutterstock.com. With thanks to Getty Images, Thinkstock Photo and iStockphoto.
Front Cover – Malivan_Iuliia, Fribus Mara, Jes2u.photo, Runrun2, Noppasin Wongchum, Powerful Design, Picsfive, optimarc.
2&3 – tcareob72. 4&5 – Daimond Shutter, stocksolutions, AlenKadr, zhykova, okawa somchai. 6&7 – heliopix, Piyaset, posterior, Prometheus72, Inked Pixels. 8&9 – Cookie Studio, WAYHOME studio, Kenneth Man. 10&11 – Mark Fisher, chrisdorney, allstars, Claudio Divizia, Sarah Marchant. 12&13 – Halfbottle, Dinozzzaver, Africa Studio, MidoSemsem. 14&15 – stuar, iamshutter, Andrey_Kuzmin.
16&17 – Maljalen, Paul Maguire, Tarasyuk Igor, Romolo Tavani. 18&19 – Paul, Roland Magnusson, Photo Melon, Petr Malyshev, Ivoha, BThaiMan. 20&21 – Eric Isselee, Valeria Vechterova, Forrest9, Gallinago_media. 22&23 – Kuttelvaserova Stuchelova, NumbSt, Pierre-Yves Babelon, Asier Romero. 24&25 – Grandpa, Scharfsinn, filippo giuliani. 26&27 – badahos, xshot, ILYA AKINSHIN, gagula, kukaruka.
28&29 – anyaivanova, Wonderplay, janniwet, Mckyartstudio, Robert Kneschke. 30 – Ljupco Smokovski, wavebreakmedia.